This journal belongs to

_____

God Gives You
Hope and
a Future

For I know the plans I have for you.

JEREMIAH 29:11 NIV

Belle City Gifts

Racine, Wisconsin, USA

Belle City Gifts is an imprint of BroadStreet Publishing Group LLC.

Broadstreetpublishing.com

God Gives You Hope and a Future

ISBN 978-1-4245-5217-7

Design by Chris Garborg | garborgdesign.com

Compiled and edited by Michelle Winger | literallyprecise.com

Printed in China.

16 17 18 19 20 21 22   7 6 5 4 3 2 1

You are the only God to be worshipped,

For there is not a more secure foundation

To build my life upon than you.

PSALM 18:31 TPT

Faithful Without Fail

Did you know that the Lord is always faithful? He is! Always, without fail, he will follow through on what he tells us. Though there may be times when our earthly eyes have a hard time spotting him working in our day-to-day lives, he is always there. He has promised to be faithful to his children, and he will never go back on his Word.

So press on. Live in hope for your future and all the beauty that is ahead of you. Be confident in what he says. Hold on to your expectations for a life to come. Don't give in to the temptation to see only what's here and now. Keep your eyes on the future hope that eternal life provides.

Keep your eyes fixed on God and the promises he has made. When you struggle to see past what's happening now, remember his Word and look to what's ahead. God has promised eternal life and a beautiful future. Rest in that knowledge today.

_____

_____

_____

_____

_____

_____

_____

_____

_____

_____

_____

_____

_____

_____

_____

_____

_____

_____

_____

Let us hold firmly to the hope that we have confessed,
because we can trust God to do what he promised.

HEBREWS 10:23 NCV

We are not saying that we can do this work ourselves.
It is God who makes us able to do all that we do.

2 CORINTHIANS 3:5 NCV

You are God's greatest work of art,
created for a wonderful purpose.

"My grace is sufficient for you, for my power is made perfect in weakness." Therefore I will boast all the more gladly of my weaknesses, so that the power of Christ may rest upon me.

2 CORINTHIANS 12:9 ESV

_____

_____

_____

_____

_____

_____

_____

_____

_____

_____

_____

_____

_____

_____

_____

_____

_____

_____

_____

_____

_____

_____

God loves each of us as if there were only one of us.

AUGUSTINE

> "The Father gives me the people who are mine. Every one of them will come to me, and I will always accept them."
>
> JOHN 6:37 NCV

_____

_____

_____

_____

_____

_____

_____

_____

_____

_____

_____

_____

_____

_____

_____

_____

_____

_____

You might be imperfect,
but you are perfectly you.

Before he made the world, God chose us to be his very own through what Christ would do for us; he decided then to make us holy in his eyes, without a single fault—we who stand before him covered with his love.

EPHESIANS 1:4 TLB

_____

_____

_____

_____

_____

_____

_____

_____

_____

_____

_____

_____

_____

_____

_____

_____

_____

_____

_____

Faith is a living and unshakable confidence,
a belief in God so assured that a man would die
a thousand deaths for its sake.

MARTIN LUTHER

If God is for us, who can be against us?

ROMANS 8:31 ESV

Forget what you heard about someone
and recognize what you see.

"Here I am! I stand at the door and knock.
If anyone hears my voice and opens the door,
I will come in and eat with that person, and they with me."

REVELATION 3:20 NIV

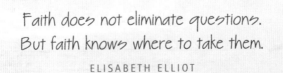

Faith does not eliminate questions.
But faith knows where to take them.

ELISABETH ELLIOT

Dwelling on Truth

Do you ever hear voices in your head that tell you you're not good enough? Do you need others' approval and opinions to give you confidence? There is good news: you are enough! God made you just the way he wants you. Those voices in your head that say you're not good enough are lies.

You can do anything God calls you to. When the voice of discouragement comes, silence it. When you find yourself desiring approval, shift your thinking and seek God for confidence. What God thinks of you matters the most.

The more you practice dwelling on the truth, the more you will see how valuable you are in your Maker's eyes. Allow him to define you and be proud of who that is. Who God has created you to be is much better than anyone you could even *try* to become on your own!

_____
_____
_____
_____
_____
_____
_____
_____
_____
_____
_____
_____
_____
_____
_____

Listen, my dearest darling,
You are so beautiful—
You are beauty itself to me!

SONG OF SONGS 4:7 TPT

You did not receive a spirit of slavery to fall back into fear, but you have received a spirit of adoption. When we cry, "Abba! Father!" it is that very Spirit bearing witness with our spirit that we are children of God.

ROMANS 8:15–16 NRSV

If you never chase your dreams,
you will never catch them.

I will bring the blind by a way they did not know;
I will lead them in paths they have not known.
I will make darkness light before them,
And crooked places straight.
These things will I do for them,
And not forsake them.

ISAIAH 42:16 NKJV

Worry does not empty tomorrow of its sorrows;
it empties today of its strength.

CORRIE TEN BOOM

He has granted to us his precious and very great promises, so that through them you may become partakers of the divine nature, having escaped from the corruption that is in the world.

2 PETER 1:3-4 ESV

Having somewhere to go is home.
Having someone to love is family.
Having both is a blessing.

The LORD always keeps his promises;
he is gracious in all he does.

PSALM 145:13 NLT

Aim at heaven and you will get earth thrown in.
Aim at earth and you get neither.

I will praise You,
for I am fearfully and wonderfully made;
Marvelous are Your works,
And that my soul knows very well.

PSALM 139:14 NKJV

Live in such a way that if someone
spoke badly of you, no one would believe it.

The LORD is near to all who call on him,
to all who call on him in truth.

PSALM 145:18 NIV

It's a job that's never started
that takes the longest to finish.

J.R.R. TOLKIEN

"Behold, I am with you always, to the end of the age."

MATTHEW 28:20 ESV

It's easy to look at ourselves and see ourselves as what we are now. God looks at us and sees what we can become.

From his abundance we have all received
one gracious blessing after another.

JOHN 1:16 NLT

Hope is the thing with feathers that perches in the soul and
sings the tune without the words—and never stops at all.

EMILY DICKINSON

For the LORD God is our sun and our shield.
He gives us grace and glory.
The LORD will withhold no good thing
from those who do what is right.

PSALM 84:11 NLT

_____

_____

_____

_____

_____

_____

_____

_____

_____

_____

_____

_____

_____

_____

_____

_____

_____

_____

_____

_____

Study a flower. Read about the human eye.
Watch the sun rise or set. Write down your dreams.
Spend some time just soaking in the
awesomeness of the Creator.

An Ideal Outcome

Hope is expecting an ideal outcome against all odds. People can put their hope in many different things, but the return of that hope won't be very successful if it isn't rooted in Christ. God asks us to put our hope in him. When the ground is shaking beneath us and things seem out of our control, we make our requests to the Lord and then believe with full confidence that he has heard.

Placing our hope in the Lord begins with giving him the desires of our heart and then truly trusting him with those desires. He honors the hope we have in him and he knows how weak our hope can be. Sometimes it's scary to place great hope in someone for fear of being disappointed. This is where we need to trust and accept that our loving Father knows what is best for us. If we hope for something that is not to our benefit, then he won't grant our request—and we will be better for it!

Hope big and trust in God. He always wants what will bring you closer to him. He wants to hear your requests and lavish you with his love. Tell God about your hopes today.

_____

_____

_____

_____

_____

_____

_____

_____

_____

_____

_____

_____

_____

_____

_____

_____

_____

_____

_____

_____

_____

May the God of hope fill you with all joy and peace as
you trust in him, so that you may overflow with hope
by the power of the Holy Spirit.

ROMANS 15:13 NIV

> Cast all your anxiety on him because he cares for you.
> 1 PETER 5:7 NIV

Oft hope is born when all is forlorn.

Do not be anxious about anything,
but in every situation, by prayer and petition, with thanksgiving,
present your requests to God.

PHILIPPIANS 4:6 NIV

The enemy always fights the hardest when he knows
God has something great in store for you.

The LORD directs the steps of the godly.
He delights in every detail of their lives.
Though they stumble, they will never fall,
for the LORD holds them by the hand.

PSALM 37:23–24 NLT

I do not get to know God, then do his will;
I get to know him more deeply by doing his will.

PHILIP YANCEY

I am sure that neither death nor life, nor angels nor rulers, nor things present nor things to come, nor powers, nor height nor depth, nor anything else in all creation, will be able to separate us from the love of God in Christ Jesus our Lord.

ROMANS 8:38–39 ESV

I find in myself a desire which no experience in this world can satisfy. The most probable explanation is that I was made for another world.

C.S. LEWIS

We know that all things work together for good to those who love God, to those who are the called according to His purpose.

ROMANS 8:28 NKJV

_____

_____

_____

_____

_____

_____

_____

_____

_____

_____

_____

_____

_____

_____

_____

_____

_____

_____

_____

Hope means expectancy when things are otherwise hopeless.

G.K. CHESTERTON

Be my rock of refuge,
to which I can always go;
give the command to save me,
for you are my rock and my fortress....
You have been my hope, Sovereign LORD,
my confidence since my youth.

PSALM 71:3, 5 NIV

Faith expects from God what is beyond all expectation.

ANDREW MURRAY

This is the confidence that we have toward him, that if we ask anything according to his will he hears us. And if we know that he hears us in whatever we ask, we know that we have the requests that we have asked of him.

1 JOHN 5:14–15 ESV

Grace is but glory begun, and glory is
but grace perfected.

JONATHAN EDWARDS

Measured Worth

Too often we measure our worth based on what we do. We label ourselves because it gives us a sense of self-importance: *I am an honor student. I am a star athlete. I am a ballet dancer.* We all have a need to know why we wake up in the morning, so we cling to labels as if our lives depend on them. If our current situation does not meet our expectations, we feel worthless and insignificant.

The good news is that we all have purpose that cannot be measured: young or old, teacher or student, mother or daughter, doctor or janitor. If we live for God, we are exactly where God wants us to be, doing exactly what he wants us to do. We don't have to go on an extravagant crusade, earn straight A's or don ballet slippers to find our purpose. Our purpose is to love God, abide in him, know him, and serve him. We just have to embrace it.

Do you feel like you are constantly trying to figure out what your life's purpose is? Stop searching and know that you have purpose right where you are. Your life is significant and valuable. Embrace your God-given purpose today!

_____
_____
_____
_____
_____
_____
_____
_____
_____
_____
_____
_____
_____
_____
_____
_____
_____
_____
_____
_____

Whether, then, you eat or drink or whatever you do,
do all to the glory of God.

1 CORINTHIANS 10:31 NASB

Let us then approach God's throne of grace
with confidence, so that we may receive mercy
and find grace to help us in our time of need.

HEBREWS 4:16 NIV

Only God can turn a mess into a message,
a test into a testimony, a trial into a triumph,
and a victim into a victory.

I am confident of this very thing, that He who began a good work in you will perfect it until the day of Christ Jesus.

PHILIPPIANS 1:6 NASB

Sometimes the only way to battle discontentment is to count your blessings and thank God for his goodness.

"If you remain in me and my words remain in you,
you may ask for anything you want, and it will be granted!"

JOHN 15:7 NLT

Today's trial is tomorrow's testimony.

May he give you the power to accomplish all the good things
your faith prompts you to do.

2 THESSALONIANS 1:11 NLT

We might be wise to follow the insight of the
enraptured heart rather than the more cautious
reasoning of the theological mind.

A.W. TOZER

Be strong and courageous. Do not be frightened, and do not be dismayed, for the LORD your God is with you wherever you go.

JOSHUA 1:9 ESV

God doesn't want you to settle for "good enough."
He wants you to go forward in life, always putting your
heart and mind in a position to learn and grow.

When I am afraid, I put my trust in you.
In God, whose word I praise—
in God I trust and am not afraid.

PSALM 56:3–4 NIV

Faith means trusting in advance what will only make
sense in reverse.

PHILIP YANCEY

Be on guard. Stand firm in the faith.
Be courageous. Be strong. And do everything with love.

1 CORINTHIANS 16:13–14 NLT

Every mistake is an opportunity to learn. To grow. To change.

Be sure to use the abilities God has given you.

1 TIMOTHY 4:14 TLB

A sum can be put right: but only by going back till you find
the error and working it afresh from that point,
never by simply going on.

C.S. LEWIS

Adored

You are like a precious flower. You are absolutely the apple of your Father's eye. He loves and cherishes you beyond comprehension. Daughter, you are *adored*. When you adore something, you don't just love it; you watch it, protect it, and handle it with great care. Your Father doesn't want to miss a thing. He wants to know every detail of your life. He handles you with such great care because he wants you to fully become who he intended you to be.

Because God adores you, he sometimes allows you to go through some things that don't feel good. But God is perfect. He is good, loving, and protective. You can trust that in those difficult moments, he is shaping and molding you to be more like him.

Can you believe that God adores you? Can you see how you have become a richer person through some of the difficulties he has allowed to cross your path? Recognize his goodness in those moments and believe that you are completely, fully loved.

_____

_____

_____

_____

_____

_____

_____

_____

_____

_____

_____

_____

_____

_____

_____

_____

_____

_____

"You are a people holy to the Lord your God.
The Lord your God has chosen you to be a people
for his treasured possession, out of all the peoples
who are on the face of the earth."

DEUTERONOMY 7:6 ESV

Let the beauty of the LORD our God be upon us,
And establish the work of our hands for us.

PSALM 90:17 NKJV

Truly, you are so many things.
But above all, you are a child of God.

Humble yourselves in the sight of the Lord,
and He will lift you up.

JAMES 4:10 NKJV

Faith is deliberate confidence in the character of God
whose ways you may not understand all the time.

OSWALD CHAMBERS

The righteous person faces many troubles,
but the LORD comes to the rescue each time.

PSALM 34:19 NLT

Light. Joy. Peace. These are things that people crave. Your influence can be in the simple, everyday way you handle yourself.

You make known to me the path of life;
you will fill me with joy in your presence,
with eternal pleasures at your right hand.

PSALM 16:11 NIV

Trust the past to God's mercy, the present to God's love,
and the future to God's providence.

AUGUSTINE

My God is changeless in his love for me,
and he will come and help me.

PSALM 59:10 TLB

If God brings you to it, he will bring you through it.

"Seek first the kingdom of God and His righteousness, and all these things shall be added to you."

MATTHEW 6:33 NKJV

_____

_____

_____

_____

_____

_____

_____

_____

_____

_____

_____

_____

_____

_____

_____

_____

_____

_____

_____

_____

Outside of the will of God there is nothing I want.
And in the will of God there is nothing I fear.

A.W. TOZER

Commit everything you do to the LORD.
Trust him, and he will help you.

PSALM 37:5 NLT

Gifts from God are all around you. Lift up your head
and allow yourself to be inspired.

Stand firm. Let nothing move you. Always give yourselves fully to the work of the Lord, because you know that your labor in the Lord is not in vain.

1 CORINTHIANS 15:58 NIV

Never be afraid to trust an unknown future to a known God.

CORRIE TEN BOOM

Equipped to Conquer

Any new situation can be daunting. A new school. A new job. A new group of friends. A new adventure. A new opportunity. Any of these could cause our knees to buckle and our hearts to race. Sometimes we need boldness for the concrete and tangible fears we face: an angry family member, a disgruntled friend, a failed test. Maybe we need boldness to defend the weak and rise up for the forgotten. Sometimes we simply need boldness to do what we know is right.

Many times, we want to cower and hide, but hiding doesn't make fears disappear. Instead, they are allowed to fester and grow. Before we know it, fear is taking control of our lives. You may wish that you were braver. You *can* be. God has equipped you with everything you need to conquer any situation. He has given you the weapons to fight with—chin up and shoulders squared. You never have to go into any situation afraid. You can have full assurance that God will give you the boldness you need in the exact moment you need it.

God made you a warrior. Warriors don't run from scary situations; they march forward and battle on. Ask God to show you just how brave you can be when you depend on him.

_____

_____

_____

_____

_____

_____

_____

_____

_____

_____

_____

_____

_____

_____

_____

_____

_____

I remind you to fan into flame the gift of God...
for God gave us a spirit not of fear but of power
and love and self-control.

2 TIMOTHY 1:6-7 ESV

Commit your work to the LORD,
and your plans will be established.

PROVERBS 16:3 ESV

Being modest takes courage and confidence. Stay true to yourself and know that what God has placed in you is enough.

The plans of the diligent lead to profit
as surely as haste leads to poverty.

PROVERBS 21:5 NIV

A God wise enough to create me and the world I live
in is wise enough to watch out for me.

PHILIP YANCEY

In all the work you are doing, work the best you can.
Work as if you were doing it for the Lord, not for people.

COLOSSIANS 3:23 NCV

The choices you make today could have
a huge impact on your future.

Wise words bring many benefits,
and hard work brings rewards.

PROVERBS 12:14 NLT

He who counts the stars, and calls them all by their names is in no danger of forgetting his own children.

CHARLES SPURGEON

Finish the work, so that your eager willingness to do it may be matched by your completion of it, according to your means.

2 CORINTHIANS 8:11 NIV

_____

_____

_____

_____

_____

_____

_____

_____

_____

_____

_____

_____

_____

_____

_____

_____

_____

_____

_____

_____

God's plan is bigger than your past.

We are pressed on every side by troubles, but we are not crushed. We are perplexed, but not driven to despair. We are hunted down, but never abandoned by God. We get knocked down, but we are not destroyed.

2 CORINTHIANS 4:8–9 NLT

How far you go in life depends on your being tender with the young, compassionate with the aged, sympathetic with the striving, and tolerant of the weak and strong. Because someday in your life you will have been all of these.

GEORGE WASHINGTON CARVER

The humble will see their God at work and be glad.
Let all who seek God's help be encouraged.

PSALM 69:32 NLT

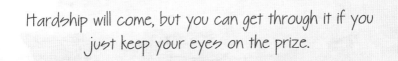

Hardship will come, but you can get through it if you
just keep your eyes on the prize.

Oh, the depth of the riches both of the wisdom and knowledge of God! How unsearchable are His judgments and unfathomable His ways!

ROMANS 11:33 NASB

It is not my ability, but my response to God's ability, that counts.

CORRIE TEN BOOM

Only One You

It is so amazing to think there is only one *you* in this entire world! Only one with your laugh, your face, your quirks, and your specific talents. No other person can be you better than you. God made you with great intention—every inch of you inside and out—and he doesn't make mistakes.

You are beautiful in God's eyes, and he created you for a purpose. The only way you can fully accomplish his purpose for your life is to get to know yourself and accept the beautiful person you are. When you do this, you wear an outfit called *confidence*. It's the kind of clothing that shines bright and attracts others to its light.

Seek the Lord and he will reveal more of who you were created to be. You may see talents come forth that you never knew you had. There is a mission for you in life: love and accept yourself for who you are. Be you; nobody can do it better!

The Lord will be your confidence
and will keep your foot from being caught.

PROVERBS 3:26 ESV

Every good gift and every perfect gift is from above, coming down from the Father of lights with whom there is no variation or shadow due to change.

JAMES 1:17 ESV

_____

_____

_____

_____

_____

_____

_____

_____

_____

_____

_____

_____

_____

_____

_____

_____

_____

_____

_____

_____

Purity is a matter of the heart. Keeping your heart pure may require you to avert your eyes, re-think your relationships, set up boundaries, and say no to certain activities.

We are God's handiwork, created in Christ Jesus to do good
works, which God prepared in advance for us to do.

EPHESIANS 2:10 NIV

When it comes to life, the critical thing is whether you take things for granted or take them with gratitude.

G.K. CHESTERTON

If any of you lacks wisdom, you should ask God, who gives
generously to all without finding fault, and it will be given to you.

JAMES 1:5 NIV

The best preparation for the future is the present
well seen to, and the last duty done.

GEORGE MACDONALD

We can make our plans,
but the LORD determines our steps.

PROVERBS 16:9 NLT

Accept God's gift of grace. Unshackle yourself from the past, and lift your face to the one true King who has set you free.

Whether you turn to the right or to the left,
your ears will hear a voice behind you, saying,
"This is the way; walk in it."

ISAIAH 30:21 NIV

The thankful heart sees the best part of every situation.
It sees problems and weaknesses as opportunities,
struggles as refining tools, and sinners as saints in progress.

FRANCIS FRANGIPANE

Guide me in your truth and teach me,
for you are God my Savior,
and my hope is in you all day long.

PSALM 25:5 NIV

Integrity is doing the right thing even when no one is watching.

C.S. LEWIS

Trust in the LORD with all your heart,
And lean not on your own understanding;
In all your ways acknowledge Him,
And He shall direct your paths.

PROVERBS 3:5–6 NKJV

Don't just say yes. It is always better to think carefully about a new venture or opportunity before you commit to it.

Listen to advice and accept discipline,
and at the end you will be counted among the wise.

PROVERBS 19:20 NIV

We are told to let our light shine, and if it does, we won't need to tell anybody it does. Lighthouses don't fire cannons to call attention to their shining—they just shine.

DWIGHT L. MOODY

Simply Delighted

Did you know that the mighty God, creator of heaven and earth, is a proud Papa? That's right! He is a loving Father who delights in you—his child! He created you not just so you can enjoy him, but so he can enjoy you.

Every good thing that is in this world is from God and teaches us about his character. Humor and laughter, art and creativity, peace and quiet, and excitement and surprises: all are a part of who he is. There are many things that he enjoys, but we are at the top of his list.

God delights in the way you see things, the sweet thoughts you have, the things that make you laugh, and the way you represent him. He delights in your hard work and determination. He adores you because he made you. You are his.

God loves you, and nothing can change that. Let that be your encouragement today!

"The LORD your God in your midst,
The Mighty One, will save;
He will rejoice over you with gladness,
He will quiet you with His love,
He will rejoice over you with singing."

ZEPHANIAH 3:17 NKJV

The Lord has done great things for us,
and we are filled with joy.

PSALM 126:3 NIV

Refuse to be average; let your heart soar as high as it will.

A.W. TOZER

We fix our eyes not on what is seen, but on what is unseen,
since what is seen is temporary, but what is unseen is eternal.

2 CORINTHIANS 4:18 NIV

If we take pride in being royalty and want to represent
our Father's kingdom well, we are more likely to make
decisions that will bring him honor.

"I will come back and take you to be with me
that you also may be where I am."

JOHN 14:3 NIV

Every act of virtue is an ingredient unto reward.

JEREMY TAYLOR

The LORD is good to those whose hope is in him,
to the one who seeks him.

LAMENTATIONS 3:25 NIV

You are never too old to set another goal
or to dream a new dream.

C.S. LEWIS

There is surely a future hope for you,
and your hope will not be cut off.

PROVERBS 23:18 NIV

You can't place equal value on shoes and righteousness;
it just doesn't work that way.

May the God of hope fill you with all joy and peace
as you trust in him, so that you may overflow with hope
by the power of the Holy Spirit.

ROMANS 15:13 NIV

_____
_____
_____
_____
_____
_____
_____
_____
_____
_____
_____
_____
_____
_____
_____
_____
_____
_____
_____

If you are not content with what you have, you would
not be satisfied if it were doubled.

CHARLES SPURGEON

Satisfy us in the morning with your unfailing love,
that we may sing for joy and be glad all our days.

PSALM 90:14 NIV

The more you choose to walk in Godly wisdom, the more Godly wisdom you will receive.

Be truly glad. There is wonderful joy ahead.... You love him even though you have never seen him. Though you do not see him now, you trust him; and you rejoice with a glorious, inexpressible joy.

1 PETER 1:6, 8 NLT